Yes, even before the world began, God had a very special plan.

First, God made a place for us to live.
Our earth, with all it has to give.

It's the perfect distance from the sun,
So we can laugh and play and run!

God made the flowers, fields, and trees.
He even made us sweet berries.

He made the sky and all the stars.
He even let us see to Mars!

God had the very best plan you see,
He even made the first family!

He made a man who was all alone,
Then a woman out of his rib bone.

The two were meant to be together,
But that's not all. There was something better.

God gave them children, a family,
To love each other happily.

But then many, many years went by.
Families were born and then they'd die.

It didn't have to be that way,
But Adam and Eve chose to disobey.

So God designed another Mom and Dad
To raise the best son the world ever had.

Mary and Joseph raised God's own Son,
Who never, ever, did one thing wrong!

Like Adam and Eve, we also don't obey,
We haven't learned, we still sin to this day.

God knew we'd need our sins erased,
So Jesus came to die in our place.

Then, WHAM! BANG! SHAZAM!
An amazing thing happened!

Jesus came back from the dead
And later went up to heaven!

God really loves you and helps you to obey.
His written word, the Bible, shows you the way.

It helps you to know Him, and teaches you to pray.
A special gift from God you can read every day!

So remember in the years to come,
When you're looking for that special one,

God has had a plan since way back when -
The best way for a family to begin.

It all starts out with a groom and bride,
Who promise they will live side by side.

This is the very best plan you see,
'cause that's how God meant marriage to be!